YOUTUBE STARS

LIZA KOSHY

Actress with More than 2 BILLION VIEWS

PHILIP WOLNY

rosen publishing's
rosen central®

New York

Published in 2020 by The Rosen Publishing Group, Inc.
29 East 21st Street, New York, NY 10010

Library of Congress Cataloging-in-Publication Data

Names: Wolny, Philip, author.
Title: Liza Koshy / Philip Wolny.
Description: First edition. | New York : Rosen Central, 2020. | Series: Top YouTube stars | Includes bibliographical references and index.
Identifiers: LCCN 2018051569| ISBN 9781725346130 (library bound) | ISBN 9781725346123 (pbk.)
Subjects: LCSH: Koshy, Liza, 1996– —Juvenile literature. | YouTube (Electronic resource)—Biography—Juvenile literature. | Television personalities—United States—Biography—Juvenile literature. | Actors—United States—Biography—Juvenile literature. | Comedians—United States—Biography—Juvenile literature.
Classification: LCC PN1992.9236.K67 W65 2019 | DDC 791.4502/8092 [B]—dc23
LC record available at https://lccn.loc.gov/2018051569

Manufactured in the United States of America

On the cover: On July 16, 2018, actress and YouTube star Liza Koshy arrives at Build Studio in New York City to discuss her show *Liza on Demand*.

CONTENTS

Some journalists and television personalities spend years dreaming about interviewing important celebrities or newsmakers. Many never get to do so or only land such an opportunity late in life. But twenty-year-old Elizabeth Koshy, known to her friends as Liza, was far from an ordinary journalist or personality.

In early November 2016, rising young online star Liza Koshy sat down with the most powerful man in the world: US president Barack Obama. The point of the video was to encourage young people to register to vote and to generally participate in politics.

In her sometimes self-deprecating trademark fashion, the quirky and funny Koshy spent as much time gently making fun of herself as she did gushing over the president. When she posted the video for millions of her subscribers to enjoy, it was slyly titled "Barack Obama Interviews Liza Koshy." Meanwhile, the fans who chimed in on her and then-boyfriend David Dobrik's Twitter accounts made jokes like, "I can't believe Obama finally got to meet Liza," and, "Omg that's awesome for Obama that's like my dream to meet Liza." These fun tweets were a way for Koshy's fans to show their love for her and acknowledge her incredible opportunity in interviewing the president.

But who is Liza Koshy? By the time of the Obama video, she had already amassed millions of subscribers on her YouTube channels, where she posts sketches, skits, and rants that she largely writes and performs on her own. Her wacky, quick, and sharp wit and ability to make fun and short content that teens can easily share and laugh over have also made her a multimillionaire, according to estimates by the website Celebrity Net Worth.

Koshy's thriving career on YouTube has led to film and television gigs, including those in web series, movies, and hosting gala events. What might be one of the most impressive things about Koshy—besides her sharpness and talent—is her savvy in a field where content creators

Liza Koshy poses at the Young Hollywood Studio in Los Angeles, California, during an October 2017 visit. Rising stars like Koshy often make appearances to promote their work.

make up rules as they go along. Koshy, along with big-name internet peers like fashion and style icon Bethany Mota, comedian and Let's Play gamer Markiplier, and others, represent an entirely new and unique kind of superstar. Some stars, like Koshy, show up all over social media, crafting YouTube videos, making tasteful Instagram entries, and posting off-hand jokes on Twitter.

What follows are the origins and story of how a self-described "little brown girl" from Houston, Texas, got her foot in the online door via the wildly popular Vine platform and transitioned into even greater stardom and creativity on YouTube. Here's the story of Liza Koshy, madcap content creator and online icon!

CHAPTER ONE

The Little Brown Girl from H-Town

Liza Koshy's story began in Houston, Texas, where Jose Koshy, a native of India, married Jean Carol Hertzler, an American of English, Swiss, and German heritage, in April 1984. The couple welcomed daughter Rachel Koshy into the world on October 4, 1987. Nearly three years later, on September 9, 1990, the family had another daughter, Olivia. Elizabeth Shaila Koshy arrived on March 31, 1996, her parents' third and final child. Liza Koshy would later joke to *Vogue* interviewer Lilah Ramzi during a "73 Questions" video, "My parents kept trying until they got the best one!"

Koshy and her siblings had pretty much an ideal childhood. Their father worked as an executive with an oil company and their mother was a yoga instructor. True to their own family story and journey, Koshy's parents encouraged her immersion in a multicultural environment from early on. Besides encouraging pride in her heritage, Koshy even attended a dual-language immersion in English and Spanish in a program she attended from kindergarten through fifth grade. It was a welcome benefit that helped unlock doors and introduced her to new friends among her city's large and vibrant Hispanic population.

A BIRACIAL CHILDHOOD

Growing up as a biracial child in the 1990s came with its own set of challenges. In an online video entitled, "Mixed Kid Problems—Growing up Multicultural," Koshy outlined how she seemed all things to all people and had problems describing her identity to friends. "People think I'm everything and anything [other] than what I actually am. People think I'm Mexican, or Puerto Rican, or Brazilian, or Colombian, or Polynesian . . . or honey roasted barbecue," she quips on the video.

Koshy is shown here at a 2015 film release after-party. Even now, people often seem to have questions about her ethnicity, which she admits can get tiring.

Her family members made it complicated, even when they were just joking around. She relates in the video, "My white grandpa would call me his 'coffee-colored granddaughter.' And my parents called me their 'little Mexican daughter.' Now if that doesn't cause a personal identity crisis, I don't know what does!" Additionally, when Koshy appeared in public with her mother, plenty of strangers would ask if she was adopted.

MAKING WAVES AT LAMAR HIGH

Koshy felt pressure to conform to others' expectations. Whenever she filled out paperwork where the respondent is asked to identify his or her ethnicity or background, she noticed how confused it made her to checkboxes that had little to do with her identity and story.

Luckily, several things made negotiating and exploring her identity easier for Koshy. One was her multicultural high school. According to *U.S. News & World Report*, black and Latinx students made up most of the school around the time Liza attended, with white students a sizable minority. She had many different friends from different backgrounds. She cherished being able to jump in and out of groups and cliques, sampling different cultures and scenes. Enriched by her friendships and interactions, she learned to take pride in her own background.

Early on, Koshy's natural talents as an entertainer shone through. She realized she had a talent for dancing and decided to pursue it. She joined the Lamar High School Rangerettes Varsity Drill Team. She later credited the experience with helping her make friends of all kinds. Even more impressively, Koshy became a lieutenant captain on the team and learned both dancing and choreography.

EXTREMELY ONLINE

Koshy's performance on the Varsity Drill Team was just a taste of how she would dazzle others in the future. Her generation was one of the first that had grown up from early childhood almost entirely online. By the time she got to high school in the early 2010s, most kids were internet savvy and used to living their lives

VINE SWINGS ONTO THE SCENE

When the Vine application and platform first launched in January 2013, few realized how big and influential it would become. Founded by Colin Kroll, Dom Hofmann, and Rus Yusupov, the platform was created because according to Hofmann, "We wanted to build a tool that would easily cut video shots together ... It crashed a lot, but we gave it to our friends and they liked it."

At first, there was no time limit for videos, but soon they realized that sharing them was much easier and quicker when the clips had a time limit. They decided on six seconds, with a half-second leeway if needed. One unique feature Vine had was letting the videos loop in place wherever they were posted, whether it was on Vine's own site, or on the millions of other sites, especially social media networks, where a Vine (as the short videos became known) could be posted.

The Vine platform quickly took off because it offered content quickly. The app's founders imagined musicians posting loops of performances, advertisers doing quick loops to sell products, animators doing very short animations, and more. They did not foresee how far users themselves could take the app. This included comic sketches, skits, jokes, and other short and sweet bursts of content. Many of these were practically tailor-made to go viral.

partly in physical space and partly online, building communities on sites like Facebook, Instagram, and Twitter.

Beyond mere pictures, blog posts, and videos, cool new platforms in the social media era gain popularity quickly if they allow users to do something new and exciting—that is, offer some new

Koshy often uses humor to break the tension of promotional appearances and networking. Here, she sticks out her tongue during a premiere screening of a film she costarred in.

functions. A major appeal of easily recording and posting video is that you can film virtually anything and put it up, free of charge, to share with friends and strangers alike. As the platforms grew, especially YouTube, thousands, and then millions, of accounts and channels sprang up.

@LIZZZA IS BORN

Koshy's friends and family had always appreciated her quirky and manic sense of humor. They also grew obsessed with the content they found and shared on Vine. Liza herself was intrigued and started her own account. She soon found that the way the app worked synced well with her own ideas, creative spirit, and comedic timing. She later told Paulina Rojas of her college paper, the *Cougar*, "I initially got on Vine because all my friends were on it and told me to join. It turned into me making funny videos in the car and things like that, and then I started making more videos because people really seemed to like my humor."

Using her real name (only with three *z*'s instead of one) as a handle, "Lizzza" was now a Vine content creator. She started posting six-second takes on life, friendship, dating, makeup, hobbies, school, snacking, and many other topics. Her wild, often wide-eyed, erratic, and energetic Vines quickly took off among her friends and then started spreading far and wide. Her Vines included impressions, observations, and even inside jokes for enduring fans, with healthy doses of physical comedy. Fans fell in love with the charming and zany Koshy. Pretty soon, she had become a minor, then a major, internet celebrity.

CHAPTER TWO

YouTube for Fun and Profit

Even Koshy seemed surprised when she won a 2016 Streamy Award for Breakout Creator in Beverly Hills, California. She was also nominated for Entertainer of the Year.

Some Vine stars rode the wave of new opportunities they encountered. Many others were overnight sensations but would later struggle for relevance elsewhere online. Vine itself had a brief shining moment as one of the most popular content-posting and sharing apps. It also shifted from a site designed to be more of a social network, where most of the traffic was generated by everyday users, to an entertainment platform, where much of the content was created by Vine power users—young people like Koshy, for instance.

It turned out that Koshy's humor resonated far beyond her own circle of friends and even beyond a few thousand appreciative fans. By the time she was leaving high school and getting ready for college, Koshy already had hundreds of thousands of followers, putting her in the top tier of Viners.

HELLO, WORLD!

In 2014, with Lizzza the Viner still blowing up, Liza Koshy the high school girl graduated and would soon become Liza Koshy the college student. Koshy decided to stay close to home and study business marketing at the University of Houston. Part of the reason for that decision was that she was still trying to see where Vine and other online creative efforts might take her.

Even offline, attention followed Koshy. Her university's school paper, the *Cougar*, did a piece on the incoming freshman class

Bringing her trademark wit and wearing a colorful dress, Koshy charmed fans and others alike at the 2017 Teen Choice Awards in Los Angeles.

a couple of months into the 2014 fall semester, entitled "Meet @lizzza: Average Teenager and Online Sensation," written by Paulina Rojas. It was a perfect headline because it underscored the many facets of Koshy's persona. She was still, deep down, just a teenager, as awkward and insecure as anyone. Meanwhile, her comedic antics were being watched on millions of screens. Her everyday warmth and engagement with audiences

YOUTUBE: SERIOUS BUSINESS

Marketers and advertisers found Vine hard to monetize, or make a profit from. The opposite has been true for YouTube, which earns profits for thousands upon thousands of companies and individual content creators like Koshy and Dobrik. YouTube allows channels to monetize their content in several ways, mostly through its AdSense program. AdSense is the program channel owners sign up with in order to get paid per clicks and playthroughs on their video content.

For example, consider the ads that play for a few seconds before you can skip through and watch the rest of a desired video. These skippable ads contrast with videos you can't skip. Furthermore, a channel earns more money if someone watches an ad all the way through. Bumper ads are also unskippable and are usually only a few seconds long. Additionally, overlay ads appear at the bottom of the video screen where content is shown and can be closed. Display ads, meanwhile, run alongside videos and are therefore one of the least invasive and distracting types of money-making ads on the site.

helped. Part of her appeal was meeting teens and other fans on their level. That same *Cougar* article by Paulina Rojas reported that in November 2014 Koshy already had 2.2 million followers on Vine.

MEET "LIZA THE LITTLE BROWN GIRL"

On July 15, 2015, Koshy went past the six-second limit and entered a new world. She posted the first video on her YouTube channel, Liza Koshy, entitled "Sup, I'm Liza the Little Brown Girl."

She hoped that Vine followers would migrate from that platform and check out what she was doing on a new one. Koshy even posted in the video's notes, "From 6 seconds on vine to almost 12 freaking minutes," commenting on the learning curve necessary to do longer-form video.

In her introductory video, she thanked her longtime fans, pointing out that many might not really know her since doing six-second clips offered little depth. Koshy told viewers that her channel would consist of a variety of content, including comedy sketches, shopping, advice, and much more. She looked forward to connecting with her subscribers even more closely than she ever could have via Vine.

Koshy got to work, promising new content every Wednesday. Most of her posts were seven minutes or fewer, to keep viewers' attention and prevent boredom.

A dash of attitude goes a long way when you have been picked as a cohost of MTV's *Total Request Live*, as Koshy was in 2017.

She was a natural at making people laugh but also found that she was great at YouTubing itself. The new style of YouTube "talking head" videos becoming popular around this time was more fast paced, with quicker cutting and editing, often done for comic effect. It all suited Koshy's sometimes erratic talents perfectly.

In addition, Koshy instinctively knew how to title and promote videos to attract viewers. Sometimes the funny titles did not match the subject matter exactly, but rather made jokes that the viewers would understand once they watched the video. The tactic was a form of clickbait, much like the saucy and salacious article headlines journalists sometimes use to make a story sound more exciting than it actually might be.

A PERFECT COUPLE

Koshy soon met someone who would become important in her life. Many YouTubers spend a lot of time fixed to their screens. When you basically live online, more often than not, you date and break up online, too. The difference for someone like Koshy is that greater numbers of people know everything going on in her life.

Like Koshy, David Dobrik was a YouTuber and vlogger. Dobrik first made a splash on the Vine platform, gaining 1.3 million followers. Koshy and Dobrik actually met via the app in 2015 and, according to Michele Mendez of the Odyssey Online, it took Dobrik four months to muster up the courage to ask Koshy out. They kept their relationship private at first. They later announced by purchasing a bunch of calendars. They circled November 28 on them, declaring it the official day they had started dating and posted a picture of them together lying on a pile of the calendars on Instagram.

When Vine shut down in early 2017, both online stars were sad to see the end of an era. Dobrik sent out a tweet, "But really I owe you a lot vine. Thank you for being my favorite dating app." Fans were touched by Koshy's and Dobrik's on-screen chemistry and antics whenever they posted videos together.

BUILDING A BRAND, BUILDING A CHANNEL

Social media stars, like their fans, are perpetually online, often via several platforms. For Koshy, whose popularity was

Koshy and her boyfriend David Dobrik were often seen around town, including their attendance here at the March 2017 premiere of *CHiPS* in Hollywood.

beginning to skyrocket in 2015, each platform was a potential asset in building her brand. In the old days, stars might have sold products. These days, many sell themselves.

Instagram, YouTube, Twitter, and Facebook all emphasize slightly different things. Humor plays differently on Twitter than on Vine or YouTube. Coupling her comic talent with her instinct and savvy about social media and marketing, Koshy was knocking them dead (in the funny bone) while realizing that she could actually make a pretty good living from YouTube. While her Instagram and Twitter accounts also grew sizably, it has been YouTube that truly put her on the map.

WHAT A CHARACTER

On YouTube, Koshy found the freedom to build complex, interesting, and hilarious characters to feature in her videos. In 2016, she began to debut a variety of characters, all played by Koshy herself. One was Jet Packinski III, who first appeared in a video entitled "Jet: The World's Greatest Olympian." The plot was inspired by the 2016 Summer Olympic Games in Brazil. Jet was really Koshy in an outlandish wig, mustache, and exaggerated eyebrows, talking in a vaguely foreign accent. It became one of her oddest and most popular personas.

Another character that Koshy often features has been Helga, whom Koshy introduced in July 2016 in a video also guest starring Dobrik, titled, "I was Kidnapped?! Helga Takeover! ft. David Dobrik." Helga is another foreign character from an undetermined nation (possibly in eastern Europe) that has been a mainstay on her channel. Helga's constant string of one-liners and jokes deal mainly with her unfamiliarity with American culture and customs.

CHAPTER THREE

From Career to Stratosphere

T he speed with which Koshy seemed to accumulate subscribers really impressed industry observers, the wider
community of YouTubers, and her own fans. According to
YouTube, on March 6, 2016, less than a year since she posted
her first video on the site, she had one million subscribers. She
had doubled that by June 16 and then doubled that, to four
million, by only September 15! On March 20, 2017, Koshy had
eight million people subscribers to her channel. The buzz
surrounding her hit a fever pitch when she announced she
had exceeded ten million subscribers on July 2, 2017.

HOW DOES SHE DO IT?

Koshy's jokes and humor are a major part of her appeal, but
humor goes only so far without something extra. Rock stars,
actors and actresses, and other superstars of yesteryear often
seemed distant from their fans, perhaps signing an autographed
picture once in a while. Nowadays, subscribers to a YouTube
channel like Koshy's are more than just passive fans. Rather, they
consider themselves part of a community. Koshy encourages
her fans to upvote or downvote new characters, sketches, and

Koshy is shown here (*center, right*) letting a fan take a selfie with her at New York City's Jacob K. Javits Convention Center in May 2017, as part of Google and YouTube's #Brandcast event.

other ideas, as do many of her peers. This gives fans a feeling of engagement and buy-in with their YouTube heroes and heroines that they may lack elsewhere. For example, when she first did Helga, Koshy asked for fan feedback on whether they would like to see the character again. A flurry of likes helped her decide to make it a recurring sketch.

Another reason for Koshy's unprecedented success on YouTube has been her "everywoman quality." She is enough of a unique voice, especially with her sense of humor, to draw attention and video views. Meanwhile, Koshy has a universal quality that appeals to a wide and varied audience. Teens and adults can appreciate something about her jokes and skits, even if her target audience skews younger.

In addition, much of her content is easily shareable, relatable, and based in every-day humor, mishaps, and slapstick. As a staff member wrote on Promolta.com, "Whether it's the struggles of impossible beauty standards, or everyone's obsession with Target, Liza creates the kind of videos that any viewer can proudly post to his or her Facebook wall."

Some content creators have gotten into trouble and faced public backlash due to questionable and sometimes even dangerous or offensive

While Koshy does "celebrity" things like attend film premieres and other events, her main appeal for fans is the sense of connection they feel with her.

videos or posts. Koshy never punches down with her subject matter. You will never see her make fun of people, mock them, try to make them feel bad, or get a cheap laugh at their expense. In a time when many online stars have been considered brash, rude, and irresponsible, Koshy is an exception to the stereotype. As a person of biracial heritage, she also knows to tread lightly and treat people of all backgrounds and identities with the utmost respect.

A BUSINESS LIKE ANY OTHER

Even before she earned gigantic piles of ad revenue, Koshy knew early on she needed extra help. When she had just left Vine and was first building her YouTube channel, she signed with Creative Artists Agency (CAA), a talent agency that represents actors, athletes, and many others. With Koshy and others, CAA aimed to expand their roster of digital influencers and stars, including YouTubers like Bethany Mota and Jenna Marbles, as well as a cappella breakout talents like Pentatonix. This was a huge development for Koshy, and it spoke to the confidence that CAA and others had in her, since she had only seventy-eight thousand subscribers on YouTube at the time, albeit boosted by millions on Vine.

In October 2016, Koshy signed another deal, this time with AwesomenessTV Network. According to Geoff Weiss of Tubefilter.com, she planned to work with them on "content development, brand deals, and to help manage her roughly one-year-old YouTube channel." Koshy was no stranger to all the perks and opportunities building YouTube fame could bring. She had already been involved in branded campaigns for products like Aeropostale, Dunkin' Donuts, Coca Cola, M&Ms, and others. AwesomenessTV's head of talent and live events, Paula Kaplan,

The cast of Hulu's *Freakish* television show—including Koshy (*seated, second from right*)—pose for a group photo to celebrate at the after-party for the show's premiere.

released a statement praising Koshy, according to Geoff Weiss of Tubefilter.com, declaring, "Liza's a triple threat—comedian, dramatic actress, and digital influencer. She has a unique ability to connect with diverse audiences, making her a perfect addition to the ATV Network."

KOSHY SCARES UP A MOVIE ROLE:
BOO! A MADEA HALLOWEEN

Few YouTubers or other performers would pass up the chance to act in a major theatrical release. In 2016, a year when other roles and opportunities came Koshy's way, she got a supporting role in a Halloween-themed comedy from director Tyler Perry. Perry had become one of Hollywood's greatest success stories with the recurring character he played in many of

Liza Koshy (*left*), Diamond White (*center*), and director Tyler Perry (*right*), take a shooting break on the set of *Boo! A Madea Halloween*, one of Koshy's first times appearing on the silver screen.

his films, a no-nonsense elderly woman with a good heart. In this newest film, *Boo! A Madea Halloween*, Koshy played one member of a group of friends trying to have fun at a Halloween party while getting into a series of comic misadventures.

Koshy was thrilled to be part of the production. Her online persona meshed well with the overall comic tone of the film. She told LAExTV.com in a November 2016 interview, "So, my initial reaction after reading the script was just 'crazy'! It was absolutely nuts how hilarious his writing is. It's Tyler Perry . . . his own voice. I just knew it was going to be hilarious."

She also felt a kinship with some of her fellow costars who were hired to act alongside her. "There are so many cast members that are influencers like myself online, and it's absolutely amazing to see that transition from digital media, and all these social media platforms, onto TV and film." A couple of the online star influencers she referred to included model and actor Brock O'Hurn, who gained fame from his Instagram account, and the actor, rapper, prankster, and vlogger Yousef Erakat.

Besides being a great opportunity for Koshy and her fellow actors, it also showed how much cultural capital online spaces now had. Online content creators on YouTube had finally "arrived," so to speak. The film itself did well at the box office and was among the most popular of Perry's Madea franchise.

KEEPING IT 100

Those who enjoy Koshy's fractured takes on modern life, young womanhood, and dozens of other topics can see that she puts 100 percent into nearly everything she does. Whether she is listing the benefits of eating in the car while pretending to crash into her garage wall, jumping around a kids' playground to deliver a nostalgic and witty look back at grade school gossip and horsing around, or making fans double over in laughter while teaching them about beauty hacks, Koshy's energy is undeniable.

As crazy and manic as some of her bits can be, she is also endlessly relatable, speaking sincerely about many topics, even if some serious ones are punctuated by jokes and punch lines. It is a delicate balancing act, because sustained fame and success on YouTube depend on being cool and talented enough to break through, while being down to earth enough to connect with fans in this digital environment.

YouTube fame also demands that creators roll with the punches, change with the times, and even change up their shtick after a while. The same things getting laughs now will be less funny in five or ten years. Koshy realizes that doing the same thing over and over again can get tiresome, too.

Koshy has also enlisted the aid of others to guest star in her videos and otherwise work with her, both to keep things interesting and to cross-network to gain other fans from collaborations. Another well-known influencer and star on YouTube, Canadian Lilly Singh, aka IISuperwomanII, has also seen big success with her vlogs, comedy sketches, and related content. Singh and Koshy did a few videos together, including "What Clubbing Is Actually Like," and have often been featured in articles together, especially ones that explore the phenomenon of young and dynamic YouTube breakout stars.

Perhaps Koshy's most frequent collaborator has been her boyfriend David Dobrik (now her ex). For a while, Koshy and Dobrik really were the most prominent "power couple" for young, always online youth. Part of their appeal, besides being two entirely different YouTubers, was the sincerity and sensitivity they displayed in their relationship, which shone through to viewers even if they were playing pranks or making fun of one another.

About a year into her studies at the University of Houston, Koshy found herself at a crossroads. She could either continue her studies in business marketing or fully embrace YouTube. One idea that involved a major change was to move to Los Angeles to continue YouTubing and explore new opportunities and collaborations in one of the two entertainment capitals of the United States (besides New York City). After thinking long and hard, she was heartened by her parents' encouragement to follow her dreams. She was especially pleased and surprised that her father in particular was enthusiastic about her potential move. With their blessing, Liza Koshy was Hollywood bound in September 2015!

CHAPTER FOUR

Keeping It Koshy

A passion for fun and helping others combine for Koshy when she volunteers for charity events, like this Stand Up to Cancer television broadcast that took place in September 2018.

Liza Koshy has hardly slowed down since she got to Hollywood. YouTube has remained the centerpiece of her success, of course, and will continue to do so. According to the real-time subscriber count via the social media analysis website Social Blade in December 2018, Koshy currently has nearly 16.4 million subscribers and counting. That success has opened up other opportunities, too, including gigs both online and off.

FILM, ONLINE, AND TELEVISION, OH MY!

Koshy's supporting role working with Tyler Perry was just one of several projects in the last couple of years. Koshy starred in a comedy called *FML*, about a guy filming his cross-country road trip with the intent of gaining a million followers on social media. Other Vine and online stars, including David Dobrik, were also in the film. Another early part she received was a ten-minute episode of a series by movie star James Franco entitled "Making a Scene with James Franco," in which guest stars join the actor in reimagining famous and iconic scenes from film history.

Koshy went a little more dramatic and creepy with another role on the web series *Freakish*, which aired on Hulu for twenty episodes from October 2016 through July 2018. Another project that featured a who's who of online stars—such as Hayes Grier, Meghan Rienks, among others—Koshy played a character named Violet Adams.

YouTube itself also tapped Koshy to do a holiday comedy special to

Laughing mid-photo, Koshy arrives at the premiere of the series *Freakish* at Los Angeles's Smogshoppe. The show ran for just two seasons but proved to be a learning experience for her.

Decked out even fancier than usual, Koshy poses for photographers at the Beverly Hilton Hotel for the 74th Annual Golden Globe Awards in January 2017.

stream in late 2016 on its new subscription service, YouTube Red, called *Jingle Ballin'*, which IMDB.com described as follows: "YouTuber Liza Koshy finds herself alone at home after her parents leave on a cruise, so she decides to throw a party and invite the whole internet. Comedians David Alan Grier and Chris Kattan rounded out a cast that let Koshy bring the comedy alongside some holiday cheer."

In early 2017, Koshy's audience expanded even more when she amused both viewers and award show attendees with her massively well-received preshow red carpet interview program for the Golden Globe Awards in Los Angeles.

SEVENTY-THREE QUESTIONS...WITH LIZA KOSHY?!

In November 2017, Koshy added another notch on her belt of fame. She wrote her online characters Jet Packinski and Helga into a sketch spoofing a video series produced by *Vogue* magazine in which celebrities are interviewed with seventy-three questions issued in a rapid-fire manner, with the interviewee having only a second or so to respond. The spoof videos caught the attention of the magazine's editorial staff, however, and soon Koshy herself in the hot seat, being asked seventy-three questions. It was yet another major milestone because Koshy was the first social media influencer and YouTuber who had been selected for the series. In other words, it was a big deal.

With her quick wit and endearing charm, Koshy fielded questions. Some of her responses follow:

Q: Best part of her job?
A: I can't get fired!

Q: Is Liza short for anything?
A: For life. I'm five feet tall. But it's also short for "Elizabeth."

Q: Weirdest habit?
A: Chewing gum all the time.

Q: Favorite hobby?
A: Photography.

Q: Heroes growing up?
A: Jim Carrey, Raven Symone—"That's so Raven" was my jam!

Q: If you had a DJ name, what would it be?
A: DJ Booth.

Q: How do you start your day?
A: Every day, I start my morning with an alarm, unfortunately!

Hired to host it by the social media platform Twitter, Koshy's livestream broadcast drew 2.7 million viewers. The magazine *AdWeek* declared it one of the most successful livestreams ever.

MTV came around seeking some of Koshy's starpower, too. The cable network was rebooting its famous television show *Total Request Live*, also known as *TRL*, in which viewers requested and made instantly famous the top video offerings of the day back in the late 1990s. The new version of the show boasted Koshy as well as other up-and-coming vloggers, including Gabbie Hanna, Gigi Gorgeous, and Eva Gutowski.

Yet another old-school classic dug up from decades ago would feature Koshy, too. The kids cable channel Nickelodeon was relaunching its family-friendly gross-out game show *Double Dare* and needed new blood for the reboot, which included pranks and lots of slime encountered by young contestants as they answered questions and performed physical challenges.

Another major project was right up Koshy's alley: *Liza on Demand*. As with her videos, the YouTube Premium web series would be all Koshy, all the time. The premise of the show consisted of Koshy doing different jobs, gigs, and tasks, as an "elite tasker" working for a fictional app, Taskit. The show was a great chance for her to showcase the style of self-deprecating and physical comedy she had honed in her own videos, drawing humor from situations that arose among friends, between Koshy and her parents, and between Koshy and the many clients whom she has to perform tasks and errands for.

BREAKING UP (ONLINE) IS HARD TO DO

Unfortunately, like many things in life, the "aww-inspiring" relationship and team of Koshy and Dobrik would come to an end. Similar to the way they announced their relationship, Koshy and Dobrik had actually been broken up for six months when they

Koshy is shown flanked by a giant poster of her during an interview at Build Studio in New York City in July 2018 to promote her new show, *Liza on Demand*.

decided to reveal the news to their followers in June 2018. Many fans were none the wiser since they had continued to appear in each other's videos, much as they had when they were actually dating.

BBC News reported, "They both admitted the pressure of their YouTube careers had been a factor in their split." It was an amicable (friendly) split. Still, Koshy's tears in a video announcing their breakup surely caused thousands more among their dedicated fans. Both of them say they may one day reconcile, but it remains up in the air. For now, they remain best friends.

GIVING BACK WITH GIVING KEYS

As Spider-man-inspired saying goes, "With great power comes great responsibility," and someone with as high a profile as Koshy is no exception. YouTubers and other online influencers often have one or more collaborations with other brands, personalities, companies, and organizations for many reasons. Koshy had no clothing, jewelry, or other branded merchandise of her own. At the same time, she wanted to do something beyond just promoting herself or whatever brand approached her. Koshy figured doing something with a socially conscious company would be a way to give back.

In August 2017, she decided to put her good name to good use. That's when she and a company called The Giving Keys announced a collaboration that would do just that. Based in Los Angeles, The Giving Keys, according to an article by Anya Thakur in the *Los Angeles Times*, "bills itself as a 'pay-it-forward' business." This means it tries to help the community. This work includes hiring people who are trying to escape homelessness at its offices and manufacturing facility. The Giving Keys' main offerings are repurposed (recycled) keys stamped with inspirational slogans that are meant to help empower people.

Koshy had to pick words that had significance for her, and she selected "laugh" and "trust," which were featured stamped on four different styles of necklace. She chose them, according to an interview with Bustle.com's Kali Borovic, "because those are the two words that play a huge role in my life—you know, other than food." She also explained her goals, "My goal has always been to spread happiness and spread some light. Trust is also a big word for me because I have learned to really trust myself and my instincts. I have learned to trust who I am." Due to the company's special mission and progressive hiring practices, Koshy was glad to partner with an organization that helped spread light by helping a community in need.

YOUTUBING 101, BY KOSHY

One great thing about Koshy's story, beyond her success, is that she has largely done it on her own, empowered by what many call a do-it-yourself, or DIY, philosophy. Many fans might want to follow in her footsteps or feel like they have their own things to say, jokes to share, or music to release into the world. Few will likely achieve the heights that she has reached, just as few will sell millions of albums like Rihanna, Taylor Swift, or Imagine Dragons. However, that doesn't mean that some people can't land a following—even a small but dedicated one—on YouTube or simply put up videos as a hobby, to have fun with friends, help build community, and even learn a thing or two.

In an early YouTube post from November 2015, Koshy provided some lighthearted takes on what she saw as common things among many YouTubers' videos. Some included typical clichés and techniques that actually work. She said:

> Somehow, on YouTube, our videos and our personalities are over-exaggerated. We feel a little more vibrant, to keep you excited, keep you entertained . . . But we over-exaggerate our intros. We're literally like online cheerleaders. The editing of our videos is often very insane, and very over-exaggerated. We really like zooming in on things, whether on ourselves, or something in the background, or just doing it for emphasis. Sometimes, it's for literally no reason!

She also talks about the jump cuts that many modern vloggers employ, in which they quick-cut different pieces of a monologue to make the narrative of the video more lively, and because, as Koshy points out, "We do it because no one likes to hear that awkward silence between things that we have to say."

Other great things about launching one's own YouTube channel can include teaching yourself how to film and edit video and audio. There are books one can buy, borrow from the library, or download that can provide instruction on how to do these things, Some of these resources are included in the For Further Reference section at the back of this book. Many online tutorials are also available, and instructions and the like are often packaged with professional-grade film editing software.

Another way to hone your skills is to join an audio-visual club at your school or in your community to bond and collaborate with other content creators. If you are an introvert, like Koshy, who has actually admitted to being so on multiple occasions, you need not work in front of the camera, either. Collaborate with friends and split up the duties—one can be a producer or stage manager, another the comedian or news anchor, and another the cameraperson and film editor.

The best way is to learn by doing, like Liza Koshy did! For now, the lessons she has learned along the way have prepared her for success in film, comedy, and pretty much anything else in the entertainment world she gets her mind set on. Now and in the future, you will likely be hearing a great deal about Liza Koshy, YouTuber extraordinaire.

TIMELINE

1996 Elizabeth Koshy is born to Houston residents Jose Koshy and Jean Carol Koshy-Hertzler, on March 31, 1996.

2013 Koshy starts to post on Vine, amassing a large following.

2014 Koshy graduates from Lamar High School and enrolls at the University of Houston.

2015 Koshy posts her first YouTube video to introduce herself. She meets David Dobrik, and they begin dating. Then she puts aside her college education to concentrate on her YouTube career and moves to Los Angeles in September.

2016 Koshy is nominated for the Audience Choice Entertainer of the Year prize at the annual Streamy Awards, where she is also named Breakout Creator. She costars in the Hulu series *Freakish* and lands the lead in YouTube Red holiday special, *Jingle Ballin'*. She interviews President Barack Obama. Her YouTube channel hits one million subscribers in March and five million in November.

2017 On July 2, Koshy reports that she has reached ten million subscribers. She does interviews at the Golden Globes' red carpet preshow, drawing millions of viewers for a Twitter livestream. She partners with The Giving Keys to release a custom repurposed key. And she becomes one of the hosts of MTV's *Total Request Live* revival.

2018 Koshy hosts Nickleodeon's *Double Dare* reboot and stars in webseries *Liza on Demand*. Koshy and David Dobrik break up but wait a few months to tell their story in an emotional, tear-jerking video post to their fans. At the 2018 Teen Choice Awards, Koshy takes home three surfboard trophies—for Choice Female Web Star, Choice Comedy Web Star, and Choice YouTuber.

GLOSSARY

biracial Refers to someone whose heritage is mixed, hailing from different ethnicities.

bumper A relatively short ad on YouTube that cannot be skipped by viewers.

channel On YouTube, this is the home page for a user's account and may be used recreationally or as a money-making platform.

clickbait Content that is presented in a sensational or controversial way to get people to click on it.

content In online terms, anything that is produced—written work, video, music, and so on—and posted to be consumed by others.

display ad An ad that runs alongside a video but does not interfere with playback or presentation.

handle The name of someone's social media account on an internet platform, like YouTube, Twitter, Instagram, and others.

immersion The act of surrounding oneself with the language and culture of a place or people.

influencer A person famous on social media who is considered influential to his or her fans or followers, often sought after by marketers to help sell products.

jump cut A quick form of editing designed to make a recorded scene feel more energetic and exciting.

livestream A real-time video or live transmission of an event online; or, the act of doing such a stream.

monetization The process of earning money for one's services and especially one's content online, such as YouTube videos.

multiculturalism A social philosophy that embraces people from many different backgrounds living peacefully among one another.

overlay A kind of ad that appears at the bottom of a video that is streaming.

resonate To affect someone in a deeply personal way.

shtick A comedian or other performer's style of performance, approach, made-up persona, or attitude.

timing The way a comedian times words and actions to achieve a comic effect.

vlogging Short for "video blogging," vlogging includes posting videos regularly on any conceivable subject.

web series A broadcast series streamed online, rather than via a television network.

FOR MORE INFORMATION

Center for Media Literacy
22837 Pacific Coast Highway,
   #472
Malibu, CA 90265
Email: cml@medialit.com
Website: http://www.medialit
   .com
Facebook:
   @Center-for-Media-Literacy
The center has been a pio-
   neer in media literacy
   education and advocacy
   and works directly to
   educate youth in media
   literacy and production.

**Children's Health and Safety
   Association**
2110 Kipling Avenue
PO Box 551
Etobicoke, ON M9W 4KO
Canada
(888) 499-4444
Website: http://www.safekid
   .org/en
This association promotes
   health and safety among
   children across Canada,
   with programs emphasizing

online safety, the threats of
cyberbullying, and more.

Digital Media Association
1440 G Street NW
Washington, DC 20005
(202) 792 5274
Email: info@dima.org
Website: http://www.dima.org
Twitter: @digitalmediausa
The association is an advocacy group for digital media
   professionals, including
   webcasters, technologists,
   and others who make their
   living online.

**International Digital Media and
   Arts Association (iDMAa)**
c/o School of Media Arts
Columbia College Chicago
33 E. Congress, Room 600B
Chicago, IL 60605
Email: admin@idmaa.org
Website: http://www.idmaa.org
Facebook: @idmaa
Twitter: @_idmaa
iDMAa is a collaboration
   among fifteen universities

exploring new and changing opportunities, including educational development, in the area of digital media arts.

Internet Creators Guild
Website: https://internetcreatorsguild.com
Facebook: @internetcreatorsguild
Twitter: @icguild
The guild bills itself as an organization set up to promote the interests of online content creators and make this new and growing profession sustainable.

MediaSmarts
205 Catherine Street, Suite 100
Ottawa, ON K2P 1C3
Canada
(613) 224-7221
Email: info@mediasmarts.ca
Website: http://www.mediasmarts.ca
Facebook and Twitter: @MediaSmarts
This nonprofit organization promotes media and digital literacy among children and youth to foster their development as digital citizens.

YouTube
901 Cherry Avenue
San Bruno, CA 94066
Website: http://www.youtube.com
Instagram and Twitter: @youtube
YouTube is the world's largest and most influential video-sharing platform, which provides amateurs and professionals alike the ability to post and make money from video content.

FOR FURTHER READING

Bernhardt, Carolyn. *Film It! YouTube Projects for the Real World*. Minneapolis, MN: Checkerboard Library/ABDO Publishing, 2017.

Centore, Michael. *YouTube and Videos of Everything!* Broomall, PA: Mason Crest, 2018.

Furgang, Adam. *20 Great Career-Building Activities Using YouTube*. New York, NY: Rosen Publishing, 2017.

Hall, Kevin. *Creating and Building Your Own YouTube Channel*. New York, NY: Rosen Publishing, 2017.

Klein, Emily. *From Me to YouTube: The Unofficial Guide to Bethany Mota*. New York, NY: Scholastic, 2015.

Mapua, Jeff. *A Career as a Social Media Manager*. New York, NY: Rosen Publishing, 2018.

Morreale, Marie. *Bethany Mota*. New York, NY: Children's Press/Scholastic, Inc., 2016.

Parks, Peggy. *Social Media*. San Diego, CA: ReferencePoint Press, 2017.

Rauf, Don. *Getting Paid to Manage Social Media*. New York, NY: Rosen Publishing, 2017.

Wooster, Patricia. *YouTube Founders Steve Chen, Chad Hurley, and Jawed Karim*. Minneapolis, MN: Lerner Publications, 2014.

BIBLIOGRAPHY

BBC News. "David Dobrik and Liza Koshy Announce Split in Emotional Video." June 5, 2018. https://www.bbc.com/news/newsbeat-44368581.

Blasberg, Derek. "Watch Liza Koshy Panic While Touching a Snake, Tortoise, and Even a Stuffed Tiger." *Vanity Fair*, November 24, 2017. https://www.vanityfair.com/style/2017/11/liza-koshy-fear-box.

Bogdanoff, Natasha, Kaila Hazarian, and Dana Stumpf. "*Double Dare* Host Liza Koshy Meets LI Kids." *Newsday*, September 5, 2018. https://www.newsday.com/lifestyle/family/kidsday/liza-koshy-interview-youtube-1.20836150.

Borovic, Kali. "The Giving Keys x Liza Koshy Collab Spreads Positivity with Every Necklace." Bustle.com, August 31, 2017. https://www.bustle.com/p/the-giving-keys-x-liza-koshy-collab-spreads-positivity-with-every-necklace-79777.

Broadway World. "Social Media Superstar Liza Koshy Signs First-Look Development Deal with MTV." August 2, 2017. https://www.broadwayworld.com/bwwtv/article/Social-Media-Superstar-Liza-Koshy-Signs-First-Look-Development-Deal-with-MTV-20170802#.

Celebrity Net Worth. "Liza Koshy Net Worth." August 9, 2017. https://www.celebritynetworth.com/richest-celebrities/actors/liza-koshy-net-worth.

Chow, Juliana. "How YouTube Star Liza Koshy Made it to *Vogue's* 73 Questions." Condé Nast Blog, November 27, 2017. https://www.condenastcollege.ac.uk/blog/2017-blog-team/november/how-youtube-star-liza-koshy-made-it-to-vogues-73-questions.

DeSimone, Evan. "CAA Signs Vine Star Liza Koshy." TheVideoInk.com, September 22, 2015. https://www .thevideoink.com/2015/09/22/caa-signs-vine-star -liza-koshy.

Dobrik, David. Twitter post. October 30, 2016, 2:53 PM. https://twitter.com/daviddobrikstatus /792846899392806912?lang=en.

Goldberg, Lesley. "MTV's 'TRL' Enlists Social Media Star Liza Koshy as Host." *The Hollywood Reporter*, August 2, 2017. https://www.hollywoodreporter.com/live-feed/mtvs-trl -enlists-social-media-star-liza-koshy-as-host-1025985.

Haylock, Zoe Alliyah. "Family Tree: Who Are Liza Koshy's Parents? Meet Jose and Jean Carol." J-14.com, November 20, 2017. https://www.j-14.com/posts/liza-koshy-parents-146885.

Heine, Christopher. "Nearly 3 Million Users Tuned in to Twitter's Golden Globes Red Carpet Livestream." *AdWeek*, January 10, 2017. https://www.adweek.com/digital/nearly -3-million-users-tuned-twitters-golden-globes-red -carpet-livestream-175463.

Hernandez, Patricia. "17 Million People Have Watched a Surprisingly Uplifting Breakup on YouTube." The Verge, June 6, 2018. https://www.theverge.com/2018/6/6/17435218 /liza-koshy-david-dobrik-youtube.

Honan, Mat. "How Vine Climbed to the Top of the Social Media Ladder." *Wired*, June 20, 2013. https://www.wired.com/2013 /06/qq-vine.

IMDB.com. "Jingle Ballin'." Retrieved October 1, 2018. https:// www.imdb.com/title/tt6291672.

@KissingNickB. "Omg that's awesome for Obama that's like my dream to meet Liza." Replying to @DavidDobrik, Twitter, October 28, 2016, 6:59 p.m. https://twitter.com/KissingNickB /status/792183951674609666.

Koshy, Liza. "How to Be a YouTuber 101!! Lizzza." YouTube, November 18, 2015. https://www.youtube.com/watch?v =4WtzkJn7fG0.

Koshy, Liza. "I Was Kidnapped?! Helga Takeover! ft. David Dobrik - Lizzza." YouTube, July 13, 2016. https://www.youtube.com/watch?v=Xn0In_mJGuE.

Koshy, Liza. "Jet: The World's Greatest Olympian." YouTube, August 10, 2016. https://www.youtube.com/watch?v=6-u9oog1nF4&t=331s.

Koshy, Liza. "Mixed Kid Problems." YouTube, August 31, 2016. https://www.youtube.com/watch?v=0q5oCema_-I.

Koshy, Liza. "Sup, I'm Liza the Little Brown Girl." YouTube, July 8, 2015. https://www.youtube.com/watch?v=H1zt7F70zEg.

LAEXTV. "Liza Koshy 'Boo A Madea Halloween' Interview 2016." YouTube, November 22, 2016. https://www.youtube.com/watch?v=IfS0tHISjoM.

Mavadiya, Madhvi. "Who Is Liza Koshy? YouTube Star Revealed after Met Gala Debut." *Daily Mail*, May 8, 2018. https://www.dailymail.co.uk/tvshowbiz/article-5703923/Who-Liza-Koshy-YouTube-star-revealed-Met-Gala-debut.html.

Mendez, Michele. "10 Times Liza Koshy and David Dobrik Were Ultimate Relationship Goals." The Odyssey Online, December 26, 2016. https://www.theodysseyonline.com/10-times-liza-koshy-david-dobrik-ultimate-relationship-goals.

Promolta. "How Liza Koshy Got 10 Million Subscribers in 2 Years." Retrieved October 1, 2018. https://blog.promolta.com/how-liza-koshy-got-10-million-subscribers-in-2-years.

Quote Investigator. "With Great Power Comes Great Responsibility." https://quoteinvestigator.com/2015/07/23/great-power.

Ramzi, Lilah. "73 Questions with Liza Koshy." Vogue.com, November 16, 2017. https://www.vogue.com/article/73-questions-with-liza-koshy.

Rojas, Paulina. "Meet @lizzza: Average Teeager and Online Sensation." *The Cougar*, November 5, 2014. http://thedailycougar.com/2014/11/05/meet-lizzza-an-average-teenager-and-online-sensation.

Social Blade. "Liza Koshy." Retrieved on December 12, 2018. https://socialblade.com/youtube/c/lizakoshy.

Sprankles, Julie. "The Untold Truth of Liza Koshy." The List. Retrieved October 2, 2018. https://www.thelist.com/95198/untold-truth-liza-koshy.

Thakur, Anya. "Liza Koshy on Pursuing Her Passion, Embracing Being a Woman of Color, and Her Love for David Dobrik." HS Insider, *Los Angeles Times*, August 22, 2018. http://highschool.latimes.com/liberty-high-school/liza-koshy-on-pursuing-her-passion-embracing-being-a-woman-of-color-and-her-love-for-david-dobrik.

U.S. News & World Report. "Lamar High School." Retrieved October 1, 2018. https://www.usnews.com/education/best-high-schools/texas/district/houston-independent-school-district/lamar-high-school-19238.

Watercutter, Angela. "How Do Viral Videos Make Money? You-Tubers Share Their Secrets." *Wired*, September 5, 2018. https://www.wired.com/story/creator-support-youtube-stars.

Weiss, Geoff. Various articles. Tubefilter.com. https://www.tubefilter.com.

INDEX

ABOUT THE AUTHOR

Philip Wolny is an author and editor hailing from Poland by way of Queens, New York. He has written numerous young adult educational texts on technology and the internet, including *Google and You: Maximizing Your Google Experience*, *Andrew Mason and Groupon*, *Foursquare and Other Location-Based Services*, and *Creating Electronic Graphic Organizers*. He lives in New York City with his wife and daughter.

PHOTO CREDITS